TRY NOT TO LAUGH CHALLENGE

9 YEAR OLD EDITION

JOKE BOOK

Silly Fun Kid publishing

© copyright 2020 Silly Fun Kid Publishing-All rights reserved

The content contained within this book may not be reproduced, duplicated, or transmitted without direct written permission from the author or publisher

Thank you for choosing Silly Fun Kid

Silly Fun Kid is a nature comedian, represents the work of comedian friends, they try to send some happiness to the little stars and make them laugh and enjoy reading jokes.

Copyright © 2020 Silly Fun Kid The content contained within this book may not be reproduced, duplicated, or transmitted without direct written permission from the author or publisher.

Have a question? please visit
sites.google.com/view/sillyfunkid/books
or
use **QR Code**

to learn more and send us message.

We hope you have a great funny time with this book if you like our books please support us with a review this encourages us to do more things.

Try Not To Laugh Challenge

 ## BONUS PLAY!

Join our Joke Club and get the Bonus play PDF!

 Simply type THIS URL :

https://sites.google.com/view/sillyfunkid/free?authuser=0

Or
use QR code

and you will get 20 best Funny jokes!
by Silly Fun Kid

Welcome to the try not laugh challenge

How to play the game?
The try not to laugh challenge is made up of 10 rounds, every round has 2 jesters, each player has a jester, and should make the second player laugh score to the points.
after completing the 10 rounds add all points and find the winner! "Master"

Round 11 : "THE ROUND GIFT"
the round 11 is the rounds gift which is the champion should get a gift!

Who can play this game?
the try not to laugh challenge is a super fun fast easy game for the family or friends to play together and get tons of laughs!

JOKESTER 1   **JOKESTER 1**

Rules of
The Try Laugh Challenge

- bring the player's friends or family members, get your pencil, prepare your comedy power.

- determine who's the "jokester1" and "jokester2"

- jokester 1 will hold the book and read the jokes.

- pass the book to jokester 2 read jokes.

- once the round completed score points.

- the same thing until round 11, then add all points to find the champion!

- all these guides you will find on the bottom the pages after.

- give to the champion any gifts!

JOKESTER 1

How do trees say hello to each other?
Thay wave!   /1

What did the fish say to her friend?
let's meet at sea   /1

What do you call a panda with no teeth?
A gummy panda!   /1

What do you call pizza that isn't yours?
Nacho pizza!   /1

 JOKES TOTAL   /4

JOKESTER 1

Where do cows go friday night?
To the mooooo-vies!   /1

What do you call a pig with no legs?
Ground beef!   /1

What do you call a cow that knows karate?
A beef chop!   /1

Why ghosts can't drive?
Because they don't have driving license!   /1

 **JOKES TOTAL**   /4

pass the book to jokester 2! ➡

JOKESTER 2

What do animal need in the sea?
Swimwear!   /1

Why do cheeps have curly hair?
Because they don't comb their hair!
                                             /1

What do you call turtle sleeping on it's back?
Yuga turtle!
                                             /1

What do you call taller hose?
Giraffe horse!
                                             /1

 JOKES TOTAL   /4

JOKESTER 2

What did math book say to other books? /1
I have many problems!

What do you call pizza without cheese? /1
Ketchup!

What do you call a sleeping bull? /1
The good night bull!

What did the W say to the V? /1
I'm double you

JOKES TOTAL /4

time to add up your points! ➡

SCORE BOARD

In each jokester's add total jokes points for this round!

JOKESTER 1   /8
                ———
                TOTAL

JOKESTER 2   /8
                ———
                TOTAL

———————
ROUND 1 WINNER

JOKESTER 1

Why do fishes swim in saltwater? /1
Because pepper water makes them sneeze!

Where do you find a lazy dog? /1
Right where you left him!

Where do sharks keep their money? /1
In the river bank!

Why did the gum cross the road? /1
It was stuck to the ducks foot!

 **JOKES TOTAL** /4

JOKESTER 1

Why did the farmer cut sheep's wool? /1
It's fashion!

Why did the fish go to the river? /1
Because the sea is salty!

How do you know if there's an dinosaur under your bed? /1
Your head hits the ceiling!

Why is horse's hair smooth? /1
Because he uses straightening hair!

 JOKES TOTAL /4

pass the book to jokester 2! ➡

JOKESTER 2

How do you keep cat from charging? ___/1
Take away her credit card!

Why did the bear paint himself different colors? ___/1
So he could hide in the crayon box!

What cheeseburger say to the hot dog? ___/1
I'm famous!

What do spiders go at night? ___/1
To the party!

 JOKES TOTAL ___/4

JOKESTER 2

What do you call a cat that can tell time? ___/1
A watch cat!

What did one party hat say to the other? ___/1
Stay here, I'm going to the birthday!

What side of a chicken has the most feathers? ___/1
The outside!

Where do the oceans meet? ___/1
In the sea restaurant!

 **JOKES TOTAL** ___/4

time to add up your points!

SCORE BOARD

In each jokester's add total jokes points for this round!

JOKESTER 1

/8
———
TOTAL

JOKESTER 2

/8
———
TOTAL

———————
ROUND 2 WINNER

JOKESTER 1

What do you call mammoths without large teeth?
Elephant!   /1

Why couldn't the giraffe sing in the choir?
Because she was the taller one!   /1

Why did the spaghetti go to the nurse?
Because he felt crummy!   /1

What did the room say to the door?
Close the door!

                                               /1

 **JOKES TOTAL**   /4

JOKESTER 1

What did the science say to the mathematics?
I'm natural!   /1

What did pizza say to the sandwish?
Dinner is on me!   /1

How do you make a orange drop?
Just let go of it!   /1

Why did the girl throw her clock out the window?
Because she wanted to see time fly!   /1

 **JOKES TOTAL**   /4

pass the book to jokester 2! ➡

JOKESTER 2

When a hen is afraid what to do?
Lay eggs! /1

When cats meet what to do?
meaw! meaw! party! /1

What did the traffic light say to the car?
Don't look! I'm changing! /1

What is the witch's favorite school subject?
Eating! /1

 **JOKES TOTAL** /4

JOKESTER 2

Why should you never trust a cow with a secret?
Because it's bound to squeal.

/1

What do sheep's order from?
Cattle-logs!

/1

What do bees eat in the cinema?
Buzzzzpopcorn!

/1

What kind of haircuts do cows get?
Mooooooooocuts!

/1

 **JOKES TOTAL** /4

time to add up your points!

SCORE BOARD

In each jokester's add total jokes points for this round!

JOKESTER 1 ___/8
TOTAL

JOKESTER 2 ___/8
TOTAL

_____
ROUND 3 WINNER

JOKESTER 1

What if you find a donkey screaming at school?
Send it to school director!   /1

What did chimpanzee say to gorilla?
Nice teeth!   /1

Why snow has not sound?
Because he's not singer
                                                /1

Why was the child swimming in his dream?
Because he pees in his bed!
                                                /1

 **JOKES TOTAL**   /4

JOKESTER 1

What has a ton of teeth but can't eat a thing?
A cornfield.   /1

What do you call a dog that lives next door?
 Your neighbor!   /1

What do kids play when they bored?
Bored games.   /1

What event do spiders love to attend?
dead flies gallery   /1

JOKES TOTAL   /4

pass the book to jokester 2! ➡

JOKESTER 2

What did the old math book say to the young math book?
I've got big problems.   /1

How do you know when a car is thinking?
When the engine is running   /1

How did the baby tell her mom that she had a poo diaper?
She sent her a poo-mail.   /1

What kind of shoes do horses wear?
Sneak-ers.   /1

JOKES TOTAL   /4

JOKESTER 2

What is the language name when your nose is stuffy?   /1
pigs language

What game do the cows love to play?   /1
farting game

Why do we never tell jokes about onions?
because they make you cry of laughing   /1

What kind of lunch do moms never prepare in the morning?   /1
dinner

 **JOKES TOTAL**   /4

time to add up your points!

SCORE BOARD

In each jokester's add total jokes points for this round!

JOKESTER 1   /8
                      ─────
                      TOTAL

JOKESTER 2   /8
                      ─────
                      TOTAL

─────────────
ROUND 4 WINNER

JOKESTER 1

Why did cheese go to the art exhibition? ___/1
Because it was cultured.

Why is it annoying to eat next to hokie players? ___/1
because they move too fast

How do you throw pigs a party? ___/1
make a cake with mud

What's the most expensive kind of fish?
A diamond fish.
___/1

 **JOKES TOTAL** ___/4

JOKESTER 1

What do monkeys love to buy at carnivals?   /1
bananas ice cream! banans ice cream!

why did the donkey laugh when he sees the big balloon   /1
he thinks its a cow fart

Why penguins are beautiful?
They farting a lot   /1

what did the ant say to the elephant it's work for
big boss   /1

 JOKES TOTAL   /4

pass the book to jokester 2! ➡

JOKESTER 2

What did the bull say when he met the buffalo   /1
What's up, man!

Why should you never trust cows?   /1
They're always farting and don't care!

Have you heard the rumor about cheese?
Never mind, I shouldn't be spreading it.   /1

Why did the singer fall through the floorboards?
He was just going through a stage.   /1

 **JOKES TOTAL**   /4

JOKESTER 2

What did the big shark say when he saw a large selection of sardines?   /1
Sardinia! Sardinia!

How do you keep a bagel from getting away?   /1
put sausages on it

What do you call a dragon roasts meat with fire that comes out from his mouth?   /1
dragon barbecue

What did the chimpanzee say when he ate the clown banana?   /1
This tastes a little funny.

 **JOKES TOTAL**   /4

time to add up your points!

SCORE BOARD

In each jokester's add total jokes points for this round!

JOKESTER 1   ____ /8
                            TOTAL

JOKESTER 2   ____ /8
                            TOTAL

_____
ROUND 5 WINNER

JOKESTER 1

What's the best thing to put into a pizza?   /1
Your teeth.

Why the old lady didn't find the broom?   /1
she goes to the birthday party

How do sea animals keep in touch these days?
SEA-mail.   /1

what did he do crocodile when he heard there is a brand in his name?
don't talk to me I'm famous!   /1

 JOKES TOTAL   /4

JOKESTER 1

What do you get when you put cheese next to some chickens? ___/1
tacos

What do you call a tired tomato?
Sleep-tomato.   ___/1

What do rats eat for breakfast?
cheese crispies.

___/1

Why do computers never fall asleep?
They like their work!

___/1

 **JOKES TOTAL**   ___/4

pass the book to jokester 2! ➡

JOKESTER 2

What did the bread say to the strawberry paste?   /1
Quit stalking me.

Why can't the music teacher go to the bathroom?   /1
The music will follow him

What do cats read?   /1
CAT-logs

Why are spiders, like shopping?   /1
They like finding bugs at low prices.

 **JOKES TOTAL**   /4

JOKESTER 2

What did the bear say when it saw the lion outside from the beauty salon? /1
nice haircut!

what did the sheep watch Friday night? /1
horror movie!

what the night say to the sun? /1
time to sleep!

How did the shark win the beauty contest? /1
brushing his teeth!

 **JOKES TOTAL** /4

time to add up your points!

SCORE BOARD

In each jokester's add total jokes points for this round!

JOKESTER 1   /8
                      TOTAL

JOKESTER 2   /8
                      TOTAL

_____

ROUND 6 WINNER

JOKESTER 1

Did you hear about the two monkeys who stole a calendar?   /1
They each got six months.

What do you call sad chocolate?   /1
A melted chocolate

What do you call a chicken with no legs?   /1
inedible dinner!

when the school gets angry, what do say?
test! test! test!   /1

 **JOKES TOTAL**   /4

JOKESTER 1

what did the turkey say when he find the cornfield?
I'm bellionaire! /1

why did kangaroo travel to japan?
he like sushi! /1

what did the elephant say when he crosses the road to the driver?
nice car! /1

What's a shark's favorite kind of weather?
water winter! /1

 **JOKES TOTAL** /4

pass the book to jokester 2! ➡

JOKESTER 2

What did the washing machine say to the clothes?
Your smell is stinky!   /1

What's a gorilla's strongest subject in school?
Hiss-tory.   /1

What kind of music do dinosaurs listen to?
rock music.   /1

Where did the mummies go to take care of themselves?
mummification center   /1

 **JOKES TOTAL**   /4

JOKESTER 2

What did the mammoth say to the elephant?
you look like me!

/1

What does the ball say when seeing the window?
Time to get a new window.

/1

whet does the pig chef prepare dinner for today?
cow dung with sheep peas!

/1

where does the time travel every time?
to the future!

/1

JOKES TOTAL /4

time to add up your points! ➡

SCORE BOARD

In each jokester's add total jokes points for this round!

JOKESTER 1 /8
_____
TOTAL

JOKESTER 2 /8
_____
TOTAL

_____
ROUND 7 WINNER

JOKESTER 1

Where does popcorn going every night?
to the cinema!

___/1

what do the dragon when he eats too much?
farting fart fire

___/1

what did the unicorn say to the lollipop?
you are sweety!

___/1

Why did the electricity go out?
she wanted to take a break!

___/1

 **JOKES TOTAL** ___/4

JOKESTER 1

What do horses eat before a race?
Nothing. They fast. /1

What was given to the loser boxer?
box! /1

Why did the Hockey player wear two pairs of pants?
In case he got a hole in one. /1

Where did color pencils invite?
drawing share! /1

 **JOKES TOTAL** /4

pass the book to jokester 2!

JOKESTER 2

Did you hear the joke about the wall? /1
Never mind, you are leaning on it.

What kind of ice cream does the polar bear like? /1
snow ice cream

What did the owl do when she heard the king lion farting? /1
he took out his eyes!

What's the difference between an elephant and a fish?
an elephant fart can cause an earthquake, but a fart fish has bubbles /1

 JOKES TOTAL /4

JOKESTER 2

which favorite party the sausages like to go to?   /1
barbecue party!

what did the lion do when he sees the doctor come to injecting him?   /1
sorry, I have meeting in the woods

what did pizza say when she saw herself in the mirror?   /1
I'm so cheesy!!

what did the red carpet say to her friends?   /1
I took a selfie with all celebrities

 **JOKES TOTAL**   /4

time to add up your points!

SCORE BOARD

In each jokester's add total jokes points for this round!

JOKESTER 1   ___/8
     TOTAL

JOKESTER 2   ___/8
     TOTAL

_____
ROUND 8 WINNER

JOKESTER 1

what did puppy say to his father when he poo
papa poo!

___/1

why the pirate are so stinky?
because they eat sticky sardines

___/1

Why can't you trust zookeepers?
They love lions.

___/1

Where do you learn to make ice cream?
ice share

___/1

 JOKES TOTAL ___/4

JOKESTER 1

Where do sheep go on December 31st?
A moo year's eve party.   /1

Why shouldn't you tell secrets in the sea?
because sharks do not sleep   /1

What did the snowman ask the other snowman?
it's snowing!   /1

How do you stop an astronaut's donkey from screaming?
You rocket!   /1

JOKES TOTAL   /4

pass the book to jokester 2! ➡

JOKESTER 2

why did all the rats go to
the garbage in November?   ___/1
for shopping, it's Black Friday!

why is it noisy on a rainy day?
because the raindrops are going to the   ___/1
concert

why did chameleon change her
color on 31 December?   ___/1
it's the new year! she wants a new look!

Why didn't the balloon sink?
It was too light.   ___/1

 JOKES TOTAL   ___/4

JOKESTER 2

why mermaids are beautiful?
they fart too much!!

/1

what is the real name of the panda?
black and white bear!

/1

what did eggs do when they birth?
cry like a baby!

/1

what did the dragon do when the dinosaur told him a joke?
laughing fire!

/1

 **JOKES TOTAL** /4

time to add up your points!

SCORE BOARD

In each jokester's add total jokes points for this round!

JOKESTER 1

/8
___
TOTAL

JOKESTER 2

/8
___
TOTAL

___
ROUND 9 WINNER

JOKESTER 1

What did the cheese do when smelling stinky?
takes a bath

___/1

Why couldn't the hen pay for dinner?
Her bill was too big.

___/1

What kind of tree fits in your head?
A banana tree.

___/1

What's sweet and bad for your teeth?
A lollipop

___/1

JOKES TOTAL ___/4

JOKESTER 1

Where do bees go on December 31st?
A bzzzzz year's eve party.   /1

What is the secret was between shark and octopus?
farting in underwater!   /1

What did the snow do when snowing?
he builds a snowman!   /1

What kind of music does fart like?
a poo pop!.   /1

JOKES TOTAL   /4

pass the book to jokester 2! ➡

JOKESTER 2

where did cows go on 31 December? /1
to see a moo fireworks

where did the golf ball disappear? /1
the hen took it, she thought it was her egg!

what does the egg do every morning? /1
she lies down in a saucer with pancakes

where did the gold medal sit in the plane? /1
first-class!

 **JOKES TOTAL** /4

JOKESTER 2

What did the mother mammoth say to her kids when they were not behaving? ___/1
Tusk, tusk.

What are sea pirates most worried about? ___/1
captain's cap disappear

What do you call old cake? ___/1
a retired cake

What happened to the barren land? ___/1
she drank all the water!

 **JOKES TOTAL** ___/4

time to add up your points!

SCORE BOARD

In each jokester's add total jokes points for this round!

JOKESTER 1 /8
_____
TOTAL

JOKESTER 2 /8
_____
TOTAL

_____
ROUND 10 WINNER

ROUND

11

ROUND GIFT

JOKESTER 1

Where did the big cake go?
to the wedding

_____ /1

where do fishes go at the weekend?
to fishing!

_____ /1

What kind of movie does the bat like?
vampires!

_____ /1

what do the teeth do when they saw food?
grind it!

_____ /1

 **JOKES TOTAL** _____ /4

JOKESTER 1

what did cockroach find in the bathroom?
ice poo!

___/1

why did the ship sink in the sea?
because the sharks have diarrhea!

___/1

What did the bunny ask the other bunny?
Do you smell carrots?

___/1

why did everyone faint at the party?
because the skunk was singing a farting song!

___/1

 JOKES TOTAL ___/4

pass the book to jokester 2!

JOKESTER 2

Learning how to collect trash wasn't hard.
I just picked it up as I went along.

___/1

Why is it so windy inside a stadium?
There are hundreds of fans.

___/1

Do you know how many famous men and women were born on your birthday?
None, only babies.

___/1

Why didn't the lamp sink?
It was too light.

___/1

 **JOKES TOTAL** ___/4

JOKESTER 2

What did the mother elephant say to her kids when they weren't behaving? /1
Tusk, tusk.

What are bald sea captains most worried about? /1
Cap sizes.

What do you call a retired vegetable? /1
A has-bean.

What gets wetter the more it dries? /1
A towel.

 JOKES TOTAL /4

time to add up your points!

SCORE BOARD

In each jokester's add total jokes points for this round!

JOKESTER 1   /8
                      ─────
                      TOTAL

JOKESTER 2   /8
                      ─────
                      TOTAL

───────────
ROUND 11 WINNER

FINAL SCORE BOARD

	jokester 1 /8	jokester 2 /8
Round 1		
Round 2		
Round 3		
Round 4		
Round 5		
Round 6		
Round 7		
Round 8		
Round 9		
Round 10		
Round 11		
Total		

THE CHAMPION IS:

_____

Congradulation!

CHEK OUT OUR

Visit our Amazon store at:

OTHER JOKE BOOKS!

www.Amazon.com/author/sillyfunkid

Printed in the USA
CPSIA information can be obtained
at www.ICGtesting.com
LVHW021041241223
767335LV00046B/1873